POETRY FOR YOUNG PEOPLE

Maya Angelou

Edited by Edwin Graves Wilson, Ph.D. • Illustrated by Jerome Lagarrigue

STERLING CHILDREN'S BOOKS
New York

*To my great-grandchildren Caylin Nicole Johnson and Brandon Bailey Johnson
and to all the sweet great-grandchildren in the world. —M.A.*

To my grandchildren Buddy and Harry. —E.G.W.

In loving memory of my grandmother Virginia "Nana" Barlow. —J.L.

STERLING CHILDREN'S BOOKS
New York

An Imprint of Sterling Publishing
387 Park Avenue South
New York, NY 10016

STERLING CHILDREN'S BOOKS and the distinctive Sterling Children's Books logo
are trademarks of Sterling Publishing Co., Inc.

This new edition published in 2013 by Sterling Publishing Co., Inc.
Editorial Material © 2007 by Edwin Graves Wilson
Illustrations © 2007 by Jerome Lagarrigue
Designed by Jen Browning and Elizabeth Phillips

Published by arrangement with Random House, a division of Random House, Inc.

ISBN 978-1-4549-0329-1

Distributed in Canada by Sterling Publishing
c/o Canadian Manda Group, 165 Dufferin Street
Toronto, Ontario, Canada M6K 3H6

For information about custom editions, special sales, and premium and corporate purchases,
please contact Sterling Special Sales at 800-805-5489 or specialsales@sterlingpublishing.com.

Manufactured in Canada

Lot #:
2 4 6 8 10 9 7 5 3
06/14
www.sterlingpublishing.com/kids

Contents

Introduction

When Marguerite Johnson—she was later to become known as Maya Angelou—was three years old and her brother Bailey was four, their parents, whose marriage had failed, sent them to Stamps, Arkansas, to live with their grandmother, Mrs. Annie Henderson, whom they called "Momma." Marguerite had been born in St. Louis but was living in Long Beach, California, when the move took place.

The year was 1931. Stamps was a small Southern town, harsh and unyielding, by custom and practice, in its history of segregation. Blacks and whites lived on different sides of town. They went to different schools and traded in different stores. Angelou later remembered that blacks dreaded whites, and that fear was heightened by the difference she saw between poor blacks and the rich whites. Read "Forgive" and "A Georgia Song" so that you can better understand what the South was like when Angelou was growing up. Or read "Song for the Old Ones."

Most black children in Stamps didn't really know "what whites looked like." Angelou once said, "I thought whites were like ghosts, that if you put your hand on one your finger would go all the way through. . . . The real people were black people."

In Stamps, young "Maya" (she was given that nickname by her brother, who first called her "Mya Sister" and, later, "My" and then "Maya") lived with her grandmother and her uncle Willie in the rear of the Wm. Johnson General Merchandise Store, which Momma had owned for about twenty-five years. The store was the center of activities in town, and Maya remembered the crisp meat pies and the cool lemonade that her grandmother sold.

Momma Henderson taught the children that they must have good manners. "Thou shall not be dirty" and "Thou shall not be impudent," she said, and so every night, even in the bitterest winter, the children had to "wash faces, arms, necks, legs, and feet before going to bed." They were required to be respectful to adults and call them "Mister" or "Missus" or "Auntie" or "Uncle" or whatever was appropriate. On Sundays they went to the Christian Methodist Episcopal Church, where they sometimes heard passionate sermons and where the church ladies shouted "Hallelujah" and "Praise the Lord" and "Amen." Deuteronomy was Maya's favorite book in the Bible. She "liked the way the word rolled off the tongue."

Maya's "first white love" was William Shakespeare, whose sonnet "When in disgrace with fortune and men's eyes" became a lifelong favorite poem of hers. But she read with an even more "loyal passion" the great black writers: Paul Laurence Dunbar, Langston Hughes, James Weldon Johnson, and W.E.B. DuBois. She was taught and encouraged by "the aristocrat of Black Stamps," Mrs. Bertha Flowers, who invited her to her home, gave her "tea cookies," and read to her from Dickens's *A Tale of Two Cities*. Angelou also remembers reading *Beowulf* and Dickens's *Oliver Twist*.

Young Maya not only read. She remembered what she read: the words, the sounds, the emotions. She began writing poems when she was around eight years old. By the time she left Stamps, after she had finished the eighth grade, she was already an eloquent young girl, and she had a love for words that later made her fluent in several languages other than English—French, Italian, Spanish, and Fanti, an African language spoken in Ghana.

In 1940 Maya, now twelve years old, and Bailey went to San Francisco, where their mother Vivian Baxter, divorced and remarried, ran a boardinghouse. The years in California were a period of growth and change: experiences happy and sad, inspiration and pain, quick maturity and sudden disappointment. She went to George Washington High School, "the first real school" she had attended; during her first semester she was one of only three black students enrolled. Then, at the age of fourteen, she was awarded a scholarship to the California Labor School, where she studied drama and dance. It was at this time that she started writing songs in addition to poems. She and her brother liked to go to the Big Band dances in the city auditorium, and they heard several of the great black orchestra leaders of that time: Count Basie, Cab Calloway, and Duke Ellington. She and Bailey, she says, became famous as "those dancing fools."

While in San Francisco, Maya also worked as a streetcar conductor, cook, and waitress, gave birth to a son, Guy, and was married for three years to Tosh Angelos, a man of Greek descent. From this union she took the name "Maya Angelou," not knowing, of course, how famous around the world that adopted name would become.

The 1950s and 1960s expanded the consciousness and developed the many talents of Maya Angelou. She became a singer and a dancer. She went on a tour of Europe and Africa as a featured dancer in a production of George Gershwin's *Porgy and Bess*. Wherever she traveled (to Italy, to Greece, to France, to Egypt, to Yugoslavia) she discovered the pleasure—and she suffered the pain—of being an American black woman abroad. She proudly heard Europeans speak the admired names of boxer Joe Louis and actor Paul Robeson, and she heard sympathetically their courageous stories. She visited the pyramids and reflected on the African slaves who had built those magnificent tombs.

Returning to America, Angelou continued her career on the stage and in cabarets: on the West Coast, for a time in Hawaii, and eventually in New York City. She sang at the Apollo Theatre: no place in Harlem more famous. She wrote, and starred in, a revue called *Cabaret for Freedom*. And, in meetings of the Harlem Writers Guild and through friendships with authors like James Baldwin, she began to write her autobiography. Although she had kept a scrapbook journal when she was a girl, now she had the distance—and the experience—to tell about her life.

Meanwhile, throughout the 1960s, the civil rights movement was gaining strength under the inspirational and heroic leadership of Dr. Martin Luther King Jr. Not long after he had been released from a jail in Birmingham, Alabama, he came to New York to raise money for the Southern Christian Leadership Conference, organized to fight racism and segregation in the South. Angelou heard Dr. King speak and immediately decided to give her energy and talents to his cause. At King's request she became Northern Coordinator for the SCLC, and she also joined other black women in creating the Cultural Association for Women of African Heritage.

Nineteen-seventy saw the publication of Angelou's first book: *I Know Why the Caged Bird Sings*. This title came from a poem, "Sympathy," by the African American poet, Paul Laurence Dunbar. It told the story of the first seventeen years of her life—honestly, sometimes joyfully, sometimes painfully, always movingly, and, almost miraculously, in the language and rhythm

of her own speaking voice. It was admired by critics and reviewers, it was nominated for a National Book Award, and it was read and studied by "ordinary" readers (women and men, young and old, of all races, in America and abroad) who claimed it as their own. Quickly, it established Angelou as a new and unique voice for African Americans, and it became a literary classic.

In the years to come Angelou wrote four more volumes of autobiography. The titles of these books (*Gather Together in My Name*, *Singin' and Swingin' and Gettin' Merry Like Christmas*, *All God's Children Need Traveling Shoes*, and *The Heart of a Woman*) are all designed to invite readers into Angelou's presence and make them eager to hear what she has to say. In particular, they suggest how much Angelou's religious faith and her spiritual outlook have given meaning to her life. And they also say that disappointment and cruelty and loss can be overcome and that people who have "traveling shoes" can "gather together" and "sing" and "swing" and "get merry."

Angelou is equally well known as a poet. Again, the titles she has chosen for her books of poetry indicate her spiritual strength even in the face of adversity: *Oh Pray My Wings Are Gonna Fit Me Well*, *I Shall Not Be Moved*, *And Still I Rise*. You can read some of her poems in this book. Read them out loud to gain an appreciation of their rare emotional power and conviction.

Maya Angelou's fame as a poet carried her to a thrilling moment in January 1993 when she read "On the Pulse of Morning" at the inauguration of President Bill Clinton, a fellow

Arkansan. No such recognition had been given a poet since Robert Frost read "The Gift Outright" in 1961 at the presidential inauguration of John F. Kennedy.

And then, in 1995, Maya Angelou read another poem, "A Brave and Startling Truth," to celebrate the fiftieth anniversary of the founding of the United Nations. The poem shows you how far she has traveled—in her "traveling shoes"—since she was a little girl living in her grandmother's store in Stamps, Arkansas. It also shows her strong belief that we can "fashion for this earth / A climate where every man and every woman / Can live freely without sanctimonious piety / Without crippling fear," and her optimism that "we are the possible / We are the miraculous, the true wonder of this world," the basis of the United Nations.

There is so much more to tell about Maya Angelou: the screenplays she has written, the movies she has directed, the part she played in the famous television production of Alex Haley's *Roots*, the honorary degrees she has received, her lectures and readings at home and around the world. Audiences everywhere greet her with enthusiasm. Her face, her body, her smile, her voice, her gestures: all contribute to the magic of every appearance she makes. Audiences know that she is a star, but they also remember that she was once a girl in the Deep South, where, amid poverty and prejudice, she heard the talk which became the music of her life: the intimate conversations in her close family, the throbbing spirituals of the church, the ironic talk between blacks and whites.

Since 1981 Maya Angelou has lived in Winston-Salem, North Carolina, where she has a lifetime appointment at Wake Forest University as Reynolds Professor of American Studies. She teaches classes of undergraduate students with the same passion that she brings to her performances everywhere.

Maya Angelou is the first living poet to be honored in this *Poetry for Young People* series which has included, among others, Edgar Allan Poe, Emily Dickinson, Robert Frost, and William Butler Yeats. Obviously, she already has a place in American literature that is uniquely her own.

Little Girl Speakings

Like most children, the little girl in this poem is sure that her parents—and her "dollie"—are better than anyone else's. She also loves her mother's cooking.

Ain't nobody better'n my Daddy,
    you keep yo' quauter,
    I ain't yo' daughter.
Ain't nobody better'n my Daddy.

Ain't nothing prettier'n my dollie,
    heard what I said
    don't pat her head,
Ain't nothing prettier'n my dollie.

No lady cookinger than my Mommy,
    smell that pie,
    see I don't lie,
No lady cookinger than my Mommy.

quauter—*quarter*
cookinger—*better as a cook*

Life Doesn't Frighten Me

Some of the things that frighten us are imaginary—like ghosts and dragons. There are other scary things we might actually sometimes see—like "bad dogs" and "tough guys." But when the little girl in the poem looks courageously at her fears, she is able to "smile."

Shadows on the wall
Noises down the hall
Life doesn't frighten me at all
Bad dogs barking loud
Big ghosts in a cloud
Life doesn't frighten me at all.

Mean old Mother Goose
Lions on the loose
They don't frighten me at all
Dragons breathing flame
On my counterpane
That doesn't frighten me at all.

I go boo
Make them shoo
I make fun
Way they run
I won't cry
So they fly
I just smile
They go wild

Life doesn't frighten me at all.
Tough guys in a fight
All alone at night

Life doesn't frighten me at all.
Panthers in the park
Strangers in the dark
No, they don't frighten me at all.

That new classroom where
Boys all pull my hair
(Kissy little girls
With their hair in curls)
They don't frighten me at all.

Don't show me frogs and snakes
And listen for my scream,
If I'm afraid at all
It's only in my dreams.

I've got a magic charm
That I keep up my sleeve,
I can walk the ocean floor
And never have to breathe.

Life doesn't frighten me at all
Not at all
Not at all.
Life doesn't frighten me at all.

counterpane—*bedspread*

Times-Square-Shoeshine-Composition

Do you live in a city like New York? Or have you been to one? Have you ever seen a "shoeshine boy"? Listen to the way he invents a sound ("pow pow") to go with his work. The rhythm makes him happy.

I'm the best that ever done it
(pow pow)
    That's my title and I won it
    (pow pow)
I ain't lying, I'm the best
(pow pow)
    Come and put me to the test
    (pow pow)

I'll clean 'em till they squeak
(pow pow)
    In the middle of next week
    (pow pow)
I'll shine 'em till they whine
(pow pow)
    Till they call me master mine
    (pow pow)

For a quarter and a dime
(pow pow)
    You can get the dee-luxe shine
    (pow pow)
Say you wanta pay a quarter?
(pow pow)
    Then you give that to your daughter
    (pow pow)

I ain't playing dozens, mister
(pow pow)
    You can give it to your sister
    (pow pow)
Any way you want to read it
(pow pow)
    Maybe it's your momma need it
    (pow pow)

Say I'm like a greedy bigot
(pow pow)
    I'm a cap'talist, can you dig it?
    (pow pow)

Times Square—an intersection in New York City where Broadway and Seventh Avenue meet
dee-luxe—deluxe; highest in quality
dozens—game in which two persons try to outdo each other in insult against the other's family
bigot—a person who is intolerant of someone else's belief
cap'talist—capitalist; a wealthy person

Harlem Hopscotch

A child in a big city makes up a rhyme to go with the game she is playing. Although life is harsh where she lives, she can overcome the problems of her surroundings, and she wins the game she is playing. Listen to the sound of her feet jumping; it tells you what her spirit is like.

One foot down, then hop! It's hot.
    Good things for the ones that's got.
Another jump, now to the left.
    Everybody for hisself.

In the air, now both feet down.
    Since you black, don't stick around.
Food is gone, the rent is due,
    Curse and cry and then jump two.

All the people out of work,
    Hold for three, then twist and jerk.
Cross the line, they count you out.
    That's what hopping's all about.

Both feet flat, the game is done.
They think I lost. I think I won.

Harlem—*in the northern part of Manhattan in*
    New York City; home to many African Americans
hopscotch—*a children's game, often played on a*
    city pavement

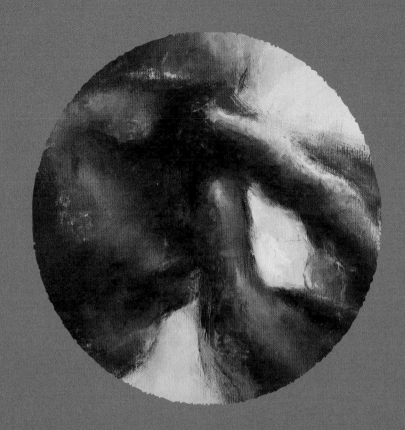

Contemporary Announcement

This is a poem meant to be sung. Try singing it. Notice the rhymes ("locket" and "pocket") and the originality of the line "Cook the cow."

Ring the big bells,
cook the cow,
put on your silver locket.
The landlord is knocking at the door
and I've got the rent in my pocket.

Douse the lights,
hold your breath,
take my heart in your hand.
I lost my job two weeks ago
and rent day's here again.

contemporary—*at the same time*
douse—*put out*

Willie

· · · · · · · · · ·

Maya Angelou was greatly influenced by her Uncle Willie, who, despite the
difficulty he has in moving, "keeps comin' followin' laughin' cryin'." He refuses to
have his spirit broken by circumstances. What does he mean when he says, "I am
the Rhyme"? Isn't that a colorful way to describe him?

Willie was a man without fame,
Hardly anybody knew his name.
Crippled and limping, always walking lame,
He said, "I keep on movin'
Movin' just the same."

Solitude was the climate in his head,
Emptiness was the partner in his bed,
Pain echoed in the steps of his tread,
He said, "I keep on followin'
Where the leaders led.

"I may cry and I will die,
But my spirit is the soul of every spring,
Watch for me and you will see
That I'm present in the songs that
    children sing."

People called him "Uncle," "Boy" and "Hey,"
Said, "You can't live through this another day."
Then, they waited to hear what he would say.
He said, "I'm living
In the games that children play.

"You may enter my sleep, people my dreams,
Threaten my early morning's ease,
But I keep comin' followin' laughin' cryin',
Sure as a summer breeze.

"Wait for me, watch for me.
My spirit is the surge of open seas.
Look for me, ask for me,
I'm the rustle in the autumn leaves.

"When the sun rises
I am the time.
When the children sing
I am the Rhyme."

◆ ◆ ◆

solitude—*being alone*

Woman Work

A hard-working country woman, with one thing after another to do, finds strength in the natural world around her.

I've got the children to tend
The clothes to mend
The floor to mop
The food to shop
Then the chicken to fry
The baby to dry
I got company to feed
The garden to weed
I've got the shirts to press
The tots to dress
The cane to be cut
I gotta clean up this hut
Then see about the sick
And the cotton to pick.

Shine on me, sunshine
Rain on me, rain
Fall softly, dewdrops
And cool my brow again.

Storm, blow me from here
With your fiercest wind
Let me float across the sky
Till I can rest again.

Fall gently, snowflakes
Cover me with white
Cold icy kisses and
Let me rest tonight.
Sun, rain, curving sky

Mountain, oceans, leaf and stone
Star shine, moon glow
You're all that I can call my own.

I've got to open the shop
Harvest the crop
Clean out the pool
Visit the jail
Get to the school
Teach all the classes
Pick up the mail
Raise food for the masses
I've got children to tend
The clothes to mend
I got to
I got to
I got to

One More Round

The man in this poem works hard at everything he does, but he is not a slave, and he has the pride it takes to keep him going. The poem is like a work song with the repeated refrain of "One more round."

There ain't no pay beneath the sun
As sweet as rest when a job's well done.
I was born to work up to my grave
But I was not born
To be a slave.

One more round
And let's heave it down,
One more round
And let's heave it down.

Papa drove steel and Momma stood guard,
I never heard them holler 'cause the work was hard.
They were born to work up to their graves
But they were not born
To be worked-out slaves.

One more round
And let's heave it down,
One more round
And let's heave it down.

Brothers and sisters know the daily grind,
It was not labor made them lose their minds.
They were born to work up to their graves
But they were not born
To be worked-out slaves.

One more round
And let's heave it down,
One more round
And let's heave it down

And now I'll tell you my Golden Rule,
A was born to work but I ain't no mule.
I was born to work up to my grave
But I was not born
To be a slave.

One more round
And let's heave it down,
One more round
And let's heave it down

grind—*hard work*

Me and My Work

Another working man—with a wife who also works and with three children to support—faces his job good-naturedly and doesn't want sympathy. He is not rich, but he has dignity.

I got a piece of a job on the waterfront.
Three days ain't hardly a grind.
It buys some beans and collard greens
and pays the rent on time.
        'Course the wife works too.

Got three big children to keep in school,
need clothes and shoes on their feet,
give them enough of the things they want
and keep them out of the street.
        They've always been good.

My story ain't news and it ain't all sad.
There's plenty worse off than me.
Yet the only thing I really don't need
is strangers' sympathy.
That's someone else's word for
        caring.

grind—hard work

Fightin' Was Natural

The boxer, a figure often used in literature, uses his fists as "a ticket to ride to the top of the hill." Boxing is a hard way to make a living, and he often gets hurt, but life outside the ring is even tougher.

Fightin' was natural,
hurtin' was real,
and the leather like lead
on the end of my arm
was a ticket to ride
to the top of the hill.
    Fightin' was real.

The sting of the ointment
and scream of the crowd
for blood in the ring,
and the clangin' bell cuttin'
clean through the
cloud in my ears.
    Boxin' was real.

The rope at my back
and the pad on the floor,
the smack of four hammers,
new bones in my jaw,
the guard in my mouth,
my tongue startin' to swell.
Fightin' was livin'.
Boxin' was real.
Fightin' was real.
    Livin' was…hell.

ointment—*salve*

For Us, Who Dare Not Dare

This tender, heartfelt tribute to the power and beauty of the African continent suggests that an appreciation for the home of their ancestors can provide positive and empowering memories for African Americans. Understanding their past can strengthen them and enable them to dare to take a stand and be courageous.

Be me a Pharaoh
Build me high pyramids of stone and question
See me the Nile
at twilight
and jaguars moving to
the slow cool draught.

Swim me Congo
Hear me the tails of alligators
flapping waves that reach
a yester shore.

Swing me vines, beyond that baobab tree,
and talk me chief
Sing me birds
flash color lightening through bright green leaves.

Taste me fruit
its juice free-falling from
a mother tree.

Know me.

Africa.

Pharoah—*King of Egypt*
pyramids—*tombs of pharaohs*
Nile—*African river, the longest in the world*
jaguars—*large spotted animals of the "cat" family*

draught—*drink*
Congo—*another great African river*
yester—*of yesterday*
baobab—*tree of tropical Africa*

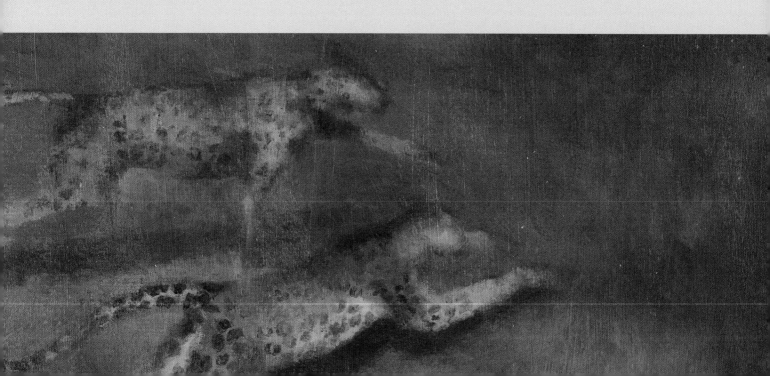

Forgive

Virginia is a Southern state. It has tender flowers, but it was built on the evil of slavery. The poet is torn between memories of Virginia's bitter racist history and the soothing beauty of the place itself.

Take me, Virginia,
bind me close
with Jamestown memories
of camptown races and
ships pregnant
with certain cargo
and Richmond riding high on greed
and low on tedious tides
of guilt.

But take me on, Virginia,
loose your turban of flowers
that peach petals and
dogwood bloom may
form epaulettes of white
tenderness on my shoulders
and round my
head ringlets
of forgiveness, poignant
as rolled eyes, sad as summer
parasols in a hurricane.

Jamestown—*site in Virginia of first permanent*
English settlement; first African slaves came
here in 1619
pregnant—*filled*
cargo—*what is being carried on a ship*
Richmond—*city in Virginia*
turban—*headdress*
epaulettes—*shoulder pieces*

A Georgia Song

Georgia was part of the Confederacy during the Civil War. There are still many sad memories of slavery in the state. But the trees, the fields, and the very names of Southern cities—Savannah, Macon, Augusta—have a music of their own.

We swallow the odors of Southern cities,
Fatback boiled to submission,
Tender evening poignancies of
Magnolia and the great green
Smell of fresh sweat.
In Southern fields,
The sound of distant
Feet running, or dancing,
And the liquid notes of
Sorrow songs,
Waltzes, screams and
French quadrilles float over
The loam of Georgia.

Sing me to sleep, Savannah.

Clocks run down in Tara's halls
    and dusty
Flags droop their unbearable
Sadness.

Remember our days, Susannah.

Oh, the blood-red clay,
Wet still with ancient
Wrongs, and Abenaa
Singing her Creole airs to
Macon.

We long, dazed for winter evenings
And a whitened moon,
And the snap of controllable fires.

Cry for our souls, Augusta.

We need a wind to strike
Sharply, as the thought of love
Betrayed can stop the heart.
An absence of tactile
Romance, no lips offering
Succulence, nor eyes
Rolling, disconnected from
A Sambo face.

Dare us new dreams, Columbus.

A cool new moon, a
Winter's night, calm blood,
Sluggish, moving only
Out of habit, we need
Peace.

O Atlanta, O deep, and
Once-lost city,

Chant for us a new song. A song
Of Southern peace.

fatback—*the fat from a side of pork*
submission—*yielding*
poignancies—*intense feelings*
quadrilles—*square dances for four couples*
loam—*rich soil*
Tara—*home of Scarlett O'Hara in the novel* Gone with the Wind
Abenaa—*a girl born on Tuesday (in the Fanti language)*

Creole—*a person of mixed African and European ancestry*
tactile—*touching so as to feel*
succulence—*juiciness*
Sambo—*unkind nickname for an African American boy*
Columbus—*another city in Georgia*
sluggish—*slow; having little motion*
Atlanta—*the capital of Georgia*

Song for the Old Ones

A tribute to older African Americans who experienced slavery and cruelty and yet survived with dignity and pride. The "old ones" kept their race alive.

My Fathers sit on benches
    their flesh counts every plank
    the slats leave dents of darkness
deep in their withered flanks.

They nod like broken candles
    all waxed and burnt profound
    they say "It's understanding
that makes the world go round."

There in those pleated faces
    I see the auction block
    the chains and slavery's coffles
the whip and lash and stock.

My Fathers speak in voices
    that shred my fact and sound
    they say "It's our submission
that makes the world go round."

They used the finest cunning
    their naked wits and wiles
    the lowly Uncle Tomming
and Aunt Jemimas' smiles.

They've laughed to shield their crying
    then shuffled through their dreams
    and stepped 'n' fetched a country
to write the blues with screams.

I understand their meaning
    it could and did derive
    from living on the edge of death
They kept my race alive.

profound—*deep*
coffles—*a line of slaves chained together in transit*
shred—*cut up*
Uncle Tomming—*being like "Uncle Tom"(in* Uncle Tom's Cabin) *whose attitude
    toward whites was regarded as servile*
Aunt Jemimas—*black women who were like "Uncle Tom" in their attitude toward whites*
stepped 'n' fetched—*reference to black actor Stepin Fetchit, who was assigned parts in
    motion pictures that portrayed him as submissive to whites.*

Still I Rise

And Still I Rise *is the title of one of Maya Angelou's books of poetry. This poem is one of her most glorious tributes to the courage and endurance of African American women. Notice how the phrase "I'll rise" is repeated more and more frequently up to the final lines.*

You may write me down in history
With your bitter, twisted lies,
You may trod me in the very dirt
But still, like dust, I'll rise.

Does my sassiness upset you?
Why are you beset with gloom?
'Cause I walk like I've got oil wells
Pumping in my living room.

Just like moons and like suns,
With the certainty of tides,
Just like hopes springing high,
Still I'll rise.

Did you want to see me broken?
Bowed head and lowered eyes?
Shoulders falling down like teardrops,
Weakened by my soulful cries?

Does my haughtiness offend you?
Don't you take it awful hard
'Cause I laugh like I've got gold mines
Diggin' in my own backyard.

You may shoot me with your words,
You may cut me with your eyes,
You may kill me with your hatefulness,
But still, like air, I'll rise.

Out of the huts of history's shame
I rise
Up from a past that's rooted in pain
I rise
I'm a black ocean, leaping and wide,
Welling and swelling I bear in the tide.

Leaving behind nights of terror and fear
I rise
Into a daybreak that's wondrously clear
I rise
Bringing the gifts that my ancestors gave,
I am the dream and the hope of the slave.
I rise
I rise
I rise.

haughtiness—*pride*

On Aging

This is another poem about the strength of the spirit. Older people should be treated with dignity and understanding, not pity or sympathy. "Tired don't mean lazy" is a good lesson to learn.

When you see me sitting quietly,
Like a sack left on the shelf,
Don't think I need you chattering.
I'm listening to myself.
Hold! Stop! Don't pity me!
Hold! Stop your sympathy!
Understanding if you got it,
Otherwise I'll do without it!

When my bones are stiff and aching,
And my feet won't climb the stair,
I will only ask one favor:
Don't bring me no rocking chair.

When you see me walking, stumbling,
Don't study and get it wrong.
'Cause tired don't mean lazy
And every goodbye ain't gone.
I'm the same person I was back then,
A little less hair, a little less chin,
A lot less lungs and much less wind.
But ain't I lucky I can still breathe in.

Greyday

A day spent away from a beloved
friend is sad and lonely.

The day hangs
heavy
loose and grey
when you're away.

A crown of thorns
a shirt of hair
is what I wear.

No one knows
my lonely heart
when we're apart.

Caged Bird

....

The African American poet Paul Laurence Dunbar wrote a poem called "Sympathy," and Maya Angelou took from that poem the title of her famous first book, I Know Why the Caged Bird Sings. *This poem deserves to be read slowly and carefully. In what it implies about the difference between the caged bird and a free bird, it becomes one of Angelou's most complex and most important poems.*

A free bird leaps
on the back of the wind
and floats downstream
till the current ends
and dips his wing
in the orange sun rays
and dares to claim the sky.

But a bird that stalks
down his narrow cage
can seldom see through
his bars of rage
his wings are clipped and
his feet are tied
so he opens his throat to sing.

The caged bird sings
with a fearful trill
of things unknown
but longed for still
and his tune is heard
on the distant hill
for the caged bird
sings of freedom.

The free bird thinks of another breeze
and the trade winds soft through the sighing trees
and the fat worms waiting on a dawn-bright lawn
and he names the sky his own.

But a caged bird stands on the grave of dreams
his shadow shouts on a nightmare scream
his wings are clipped and his feet are tied
so he opens his throat to sing.

The caged bird sings
with a fearful trill
of things unknown
but longed for still
and his tune is heard
on the distant hill
for the caged bird
sings of freedom.

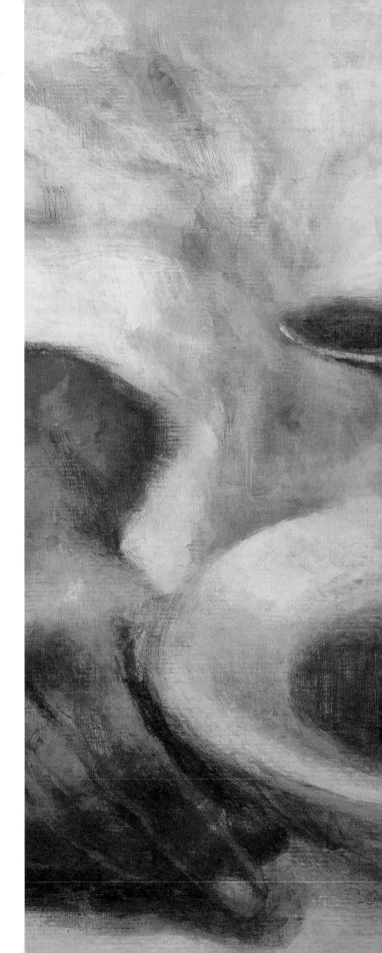

This Winter Day

Isn't it good to sit in a kitchen and watch the soup
cooking and smell it and look forward to eating it?

    The kitchen is its readiness
    white green and orange things
    leak their blood selves in the soup.

    Ritual sacrifice that snaps
    an odor at my nose and starts
    my tongue to march
    slipping in the liquid of its drip.

    The day, silver striped
    in rain, is balked against
    my window and the soup.

The New House
....

What would it be like to move into a new home?
Would you wonder about the people who used to
live there? Would you think about what you might
some day—when you move—leave behind?

What words
have smashed against
these walls,
crashed up and down these
halls,
lain mute and then drained
their meanings out and into
these floors?

What feelings, long since
dead,
streamed vague yearnings
below this ceiling
light?
In some dimension,
which I cannot know,
the shadows of
another still exist. I bring my
memories, held too long in check,
to let them here shoulder
space and place to be.

And when I leave to
find another house,
I wonder, what among
these shades will be
left of me.

Ailey, Baldwin, Floyd, Killens, and Mayfield

A memorial tribute to five African American men: Alvin Ailey (actor, dancer, and choreographer); James Baldwin (novelist, essayist, and playwright); Samuel A. Floyd Jr. (music professor and educational administrator); John Oliver Killens (author and professor); and Julian Mayfield (actor and writer). They were like great trees, and, when they died, Angelou suggests, the world was shaken by fear.

When great trees fall,
rocks on distant hills shudder,
lions hunker down
in tall grasses,
and even elephants
lumber after safety.

When great trees fall
in forests,
small things recoil into silence,
their senses
eroded beyond fear.

When great souls die,
the air around us becomes
light, rare, sterile.
We breathe, briefly.
Our eyes, briefly,
see with
a hurtful clarity.
Our memory, suddenly sharpened,
examines,
gnaws on kind words
unsaid,
promised walks
never taken.

Great souls die and
our reality, bound to
them, takes leave of us.
Our souls,
dependent upon their
nurture,
now shrink, wizened.
Our minds, formed
and informed by their
radiance,
fall away.
We are not so much maddened
as reduced to the unutterable ignorance
of dark, cold
caves.

And when great souls die,
after a period peace blooms,
slowly and always
irregularly. Spaces fill
with a kind of
soothing electric vibration.
Our senses, restored, never
to be the same, whisper to us.
They existed. They existed.
We can be. Be and be
better. For they existed.

hunker—*take shelter*
sterile—*not producing life*
wizened—*dried up*

Preacher, Don't Send Me

The speaker tells the preacher that she wants a heaven that is better than what she has known on earth. She hopes that in paradise people will be nice and jazz music will be playing. Since she is a church-goer, she remembers that when God said, "Whom shall I send?" Isaiah said, "Here am I; send me."

Preacher, don't send me
when I die
to some big ghetto
in the sky
where rats eat cats
of the leopard type
and Sunday brunch
is grits and tripe.

I've known those rats
I've seen them kill
and grits I've had
would make a hill,
or maybe a mountain,
so what I need
from you on Sunday
is a different creed.

Preacher, please don't
promise me
streets of gold
and milk for free.
I stopped all milk
at four years old
and once I'm dead
I won't need gold.

I'd call a place
pure paradise
where families are loyal
and strangers are nice,
where the music is jazz
and the season is fall.
Promise me that
or nothing at all.

ghetto—*a section of a city in which members of a minority group live separately from other citizens*
tripe—*food made from the stomach of an animal like a sheep or goat or cow*

A Conceit

. . . .

The poet wants you to take her hand and walk with her beyond the poem into life itself. Do you know what she means by "this rage of poetry"?

Give me your hand.

Make room for me
to lead and follow
you
beyond this rage of poetry.

Let others have
the privacy of
touching words
and love of loss
of love.

For me
Give me your hand.

A Brave and Startling Truth

This is the poem Maya Angelou wrote for the 50th Anniversary of the United Nations and read in San Francisco on June 26, 1995. Read it carefully, learn all the words you don't know, see how it is put together, and try to understand what she means when she keeps saying, "When we come to it."

We, this people, on a small and lonely planet
Traveling through casual space
Past aloof stars, across the way of indifferent suns
To a destination where all signs tell us
It is possible and imperative that we learn
A brave and startling truth

And when we come to it
To the day of peacemaking
When we release our fingers
From fists of hostility
And allow the pure air to cool our palms

When we come to it
When the curtain falls on the minstrel show of hate
And faces sooted with scorn are scrubbed clean
When battlefields and coliseum
No longer rake our unique and particular
     sons and daughters
Up with the bruised and bloody grass
To lie in identical plots in foreign soil

When the rapacious storming of the churches
The screaming racket in the temples have ceased
When the pennants are waving gaily
When the banners of the world tremble
Stoutly in the good, clean breeze

When we come to it
When we let the rifles fall from our shoulders
And children dress their dolls in flags of truce
When land mines of death have been removed
And the aged can walk into evenings of peace
When religious ritual is not perfumed
By the incense of burning flesh
And childhood dreams are not kicked awake
By nightmares of abuse

When we come to it
Then we will confess that not the Pyramids
With their stones set in mysterious perfection
Nor the Gardens of Babylon
Hanging as eternal beauty
In our collective memory
Not the Grand Canyon
Kindled into delicious color
By western sunsets

Nor the Danube, flowing its blue soul into Europe
Not the sacred peak of Mount Fuji
Stretching to the Rising Sun
Neither Father Amazon nor Mother Mississippi who,
     without favor,
Nurture all creatures in the depths and on the shores
These are not the only wonders of the world

When we come to it
We, this people, on this minuscule and kithless globe
Who reach daily for the bomb, the blade
    and the dagger
Yet who petition in the dark for tokens of peace
We, this people, on this mote of matter
In whose mouths abide cankerous words
Which challenge our very existence
Yet out of those same mouths
Come songs of such exquisite sweetness
That the heart falters in its labor
And the body is quieted in awe

We, this people, on this small and drifting planet
Whose hands can strike with such abandon
That, in a twinkling, life is sapped from the living
Yet those same hands can touch with such healing,
    irresistible tenderness,

That the haughty neck is happy to bow
And the proud back is glad to bend
Out of such chaos, of such contradiction
We learn that we are neither devils nor divines

When we come to it
We, this people, on this wayward, floating body
Created on this earth, of this earth
Have the power to fashion for this earth
A climate where every man and every woman
Can live freely without sanctimonious piety
Without crippling fear

When we come to it
We must confess that we are the possible
We are the miraculous, the true wonder of this world
That is when, and only when
We come to it.

casual—*happening by chance*
aloof—*distant; indifferent*
destination—*the place to which one is going*
imperative—*necessary*
hostility—*hatred*
minstrel show—*a stage entertainment using dialogue, song
    and dance and sometimes featuring performers in blackface*
sooted—*covered with black*
coliseum—*stadium*
rapacious—*greedy*
pennants—*long flags*
truce—*an agreement for a cease-fire*
incense—*perfume or smoke coming from a burning substance*
Pyramids—*tombs of Egyptian kings*
Gardens of Babylon—*one of the wonders of the ancient world*
Grand Canyon—*a gorge of the Colorado River in northern
    Arizona*
Danube—*a river in central and southeastern Europe*
Mount Fuji—*Fujiyaya, the highest mountain in Japan*

Rising Sun—*an image of Japan*
Amazon—*a river in South America*
Mississippi—*a river in the United States*
nurture—*to feed and protect*
miniscule—*very small*
kithless—*without neighbors or relatives*
mote—*a small pack*
cankerous—*causing sores and disease*
exquisite—*beautiful*
falters—*stumbles*
awe—*wonder*
sapped—*drained away*
haughty—*proud*
chaos—*complete confusion*
contradiction—*opposition*
wayward—*turning away from what is right*
sanctimonious—*falsely religious*
piety—*devoutness*
miraculous—*performed by some power outside nature*

Glory Falls

This poem has its origins in Good Friday, when Jesus died on the Cross, and in the Easter resurrection. It tells us that life is filled with sorrow and tears and hatred, but we can learn honor and we can "grow" toward a better tomorrow.

Glory falls around us
as we sob
a dirge of
desolation on the Cross
and hatred is the ballast of
the rock
    which lies upon our necks
    and underfoot.
We have woven
    robes of silk
    and clothed our nakedness
    with tapestry.
From crawling on this
    murky planet's floor
    we soar beyond the
    birds and
    through the clouds
    and edge our way from hate
    and blind despair and
    bring honor
    to our brothers, and to our sisters cheer.
We grow despite the
    horror that we feed
    upon our own
    tomorrow.
We grow.

dirge—*funeral song*
desolation—*loneliness and sorrow*
ballast—*material that provides stability*

Index